Copyright Page

© 2026 D.M.Thomas

All rights reserved.

No part of this book may be reproduced, stored in a retrieval system, or transmitted in any form or by any means, electronic, mechanical, photocopying, recording or otherwise, without prior written permission of the author.

First published 2026

Written by D.M.Thomas

Printed in the United Kingdom

# Meet Trifle!

He's a bouncy, happy dog who loves rolling in the grass and making new friends.

Written By
D.M.Thomas

Lilly and Leo were on their way to school one glorious, sunny Monday morning. They skipped and ran through the park, laughing. They came across a little dog that was trotting towards them, wagging his tail.

He rolled onto his back for a fuss and a belly rub. "What's your name?" Lilly asked. "Are you alone?" Leo wondered.
Lilly and Leo's mummy walked past, "Come along, children - you shall be late for school!"

The little dog didn't want Lilly and Leo to go. The dog softly whimpered as the children walked off to school.
"Well," Leo sighed, "that was a lovely dog."
"Yes," Lilly giggled, "he looked like a trifle, all different colours!"

The next morning, Lilly and Leo asked, "Mummy, can we walk through the park again on the way to school?" "Yessssssss!" she laughed. "It's a lovely Tuesday. Let's do that!"

They whispered to each other… "I hope we see that dog again - the one that looks like a trifle!" They laughed.

With their summer jackets on and bags ready, they rushed to the door.
"Come on, Mummy! We need to get to the park - ooops, we mean school!"
No sooner had they reached the park entrance... there he was!
The same dog, waiting for them, tail wagging wildly.

"Mummy! Mummy! It's Trifle!" they shouted. "Trifle?"

Mummy laughed. "What a funny name for a dog!"

"But look," Lilly said, "he really DOES look like a trifle!" They all giggled.

"Mummy," Leo said softly, "he has no owner. This is the second day he's been here alone. Can we keep him?"

"I'm sure his owner is somewhere in the park, We have to wait and make sure we do the right thing," Mummy said gently.

The children's faces fell as they waved goodbye to Trifle again.

Day after day, Trifle waited for them at the park gate, hoping to be taken to a loving home. Day after day, Lilly and Leo grew sadder each time they walked away. Trifle didn't understand why everyone always left.

Then one weekend morning, Mummy called out, "Come on, you two, we're heading to the park.
And look what's in my hand!"
She held out a lead.

Lilly and Leo gasped. "Does this mean...?"
Mummy smiled.
"Yes. This means we're going to pick up Trifle. He seems to have no family... and I know two little people who would give him a wonderful life."

So they eagerly ran all the way to the park, shouting:
"Trifle! Trifle! You're coming HOME!"

But as they were heading towards the gate, they heard barking and whimpering behind them!..
And to their surprise...

There stood four more pups.
Trifle's siblings...
Doughnut, Brownie, Sticky Toffee and Lemon Drizzle.

"Looks like we've got a whole bakery of pups!" said Mummy. Both Lilly and Leo burst with laughter.

"Mummy," Leo sighed, "what about Doughnut, Brownie, Sticky Toffee and Lemon Drizzle? They can't stay here all alone!"

Mummy smiled.

"Dont you worry. I've already spoken to some neighbours. Everyone wants to meet the bakery pups!" and help give the pups a loving home.

The neighbours peeked out of their windows as the pups arrived, wagging and wobbling like fresh treats on a tray.
One said "Goodness me! It looks like you've brought us all a whole dessert menu!"

One by one, Doughnut, Sticky Toffee, Brownie, and Lemon Drizzle found loving homes with families who lived just a street away, close enough for Lilly, Leo and Trifle to visit them every day.

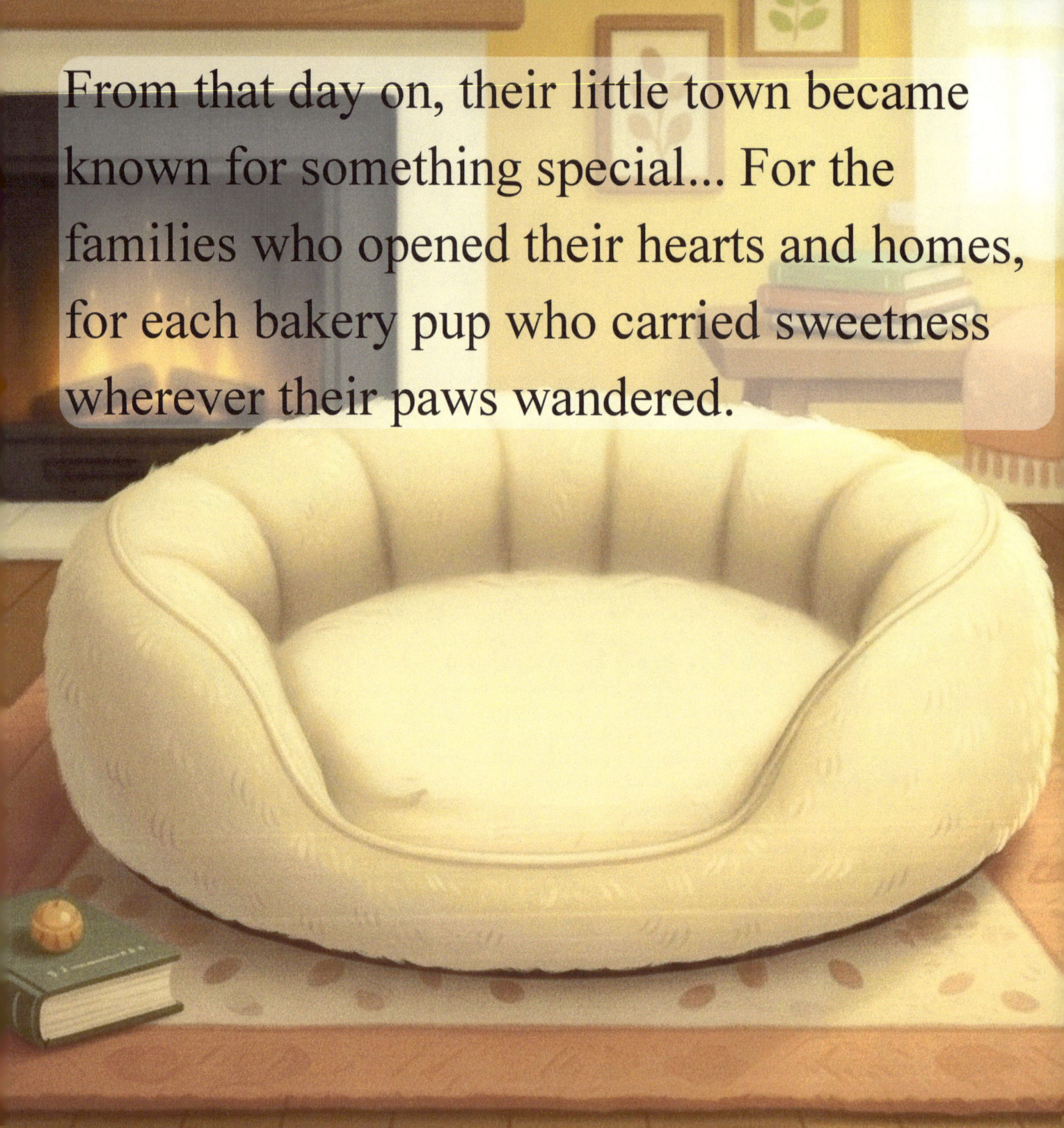

From that day on, their little town became known for something special... For the families who opened their hearts and homes, for each bakery pup who carried sweetness wherever their paws wandered.

Trifle curled up in his soft cosy bed, just where he belonged. The sweetest pup of them all. The End... or is it?

The story may be finished, but the journey doesn't stop here...
Turn the page to explore, answer questions and share your own story.

# Understanding the Story

1. How do you think Trifle felt, before he found his family?
2. How do you think Trifle felt once he was welcomed into his new home?
3. How do you think Lilly and Leo felt when they got to bring Trifle home?
4. Who is your favourite Bakery pup? and why?
5. What is one kind thing you can do for someone today?
6. Have you ever felt nervous or unsure like Trifle, and what helped you feel better?

# Can you remember

1. How many different coloured balls did Trifle have?
2. Can you remember the colours of the balls?
3. Can you remember the name of all the bakery pups?

Trifle went to bed each night dreaming of new adventures. I wonder what your dream might be tonight, or what adventure you would like to imagine?
Tell your grown up in the morning.

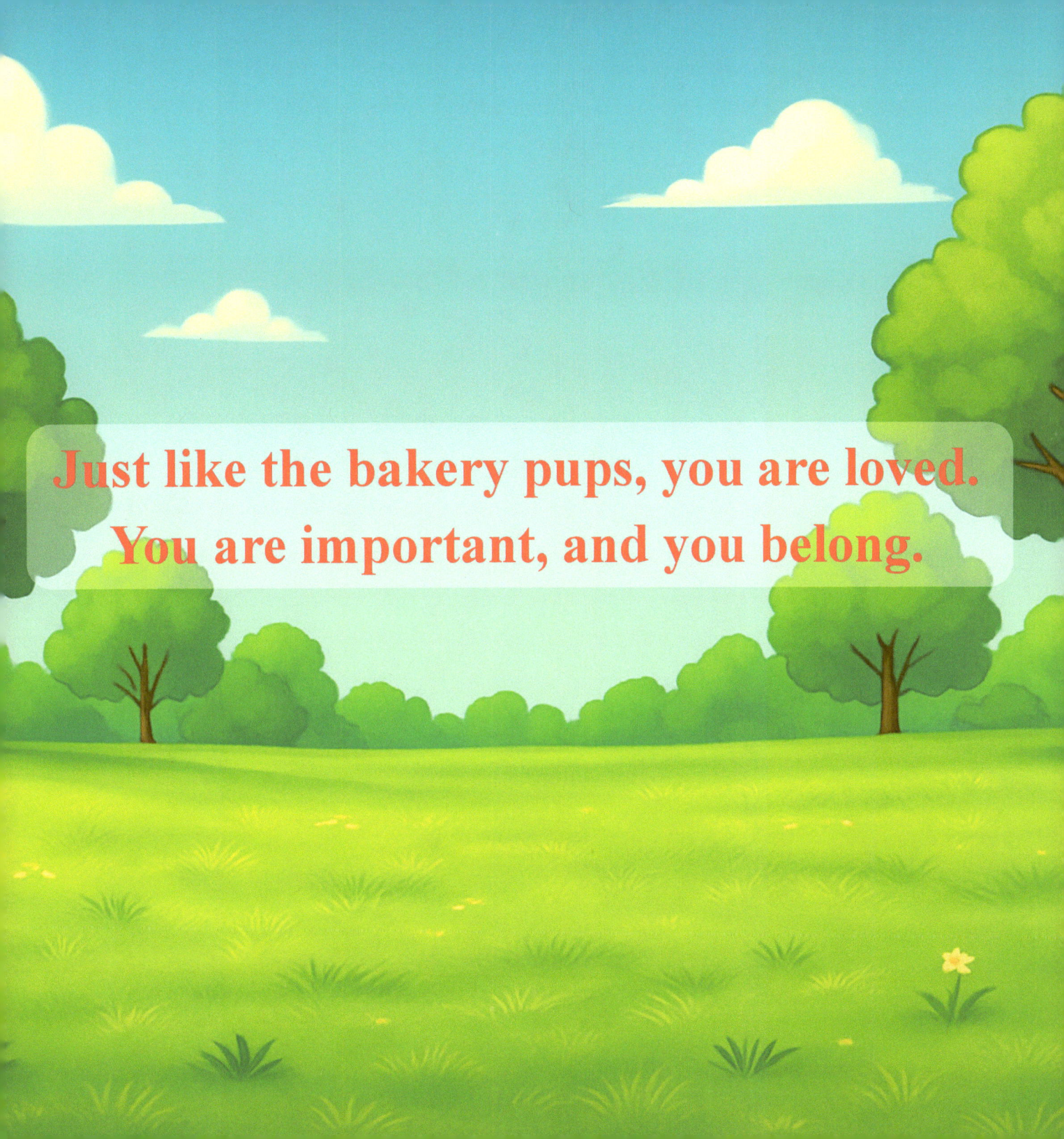

Just like the bakery pups, you are loved.
You are important, and you belong.